Northern Portrait

Northern Portrait

Poems by

Fredric Hildebrand

Cover design by Shay Culligan

Cover photograph by Charlie Hildebrand

ISBN: 978-1-952326-41-7

Kelsay Books
502 South 1040 East, A-119
American Fork, Utah, 84003

To my wife Sarah, for her patience and love,
and to my poet mentors,
Tom Montag, Karla Huston, and Peggy Turnbull

Acknowledgments

My thanks to the editors of the following publications where some of the poems in this collection first appeared, sometimes in slightly different versions:

Avalon Literary Review: "Driving Up North"

Finishing Line Press: "At a Bend in the Road," "At the Polling Place"

Millwork: "At the Ojibwa All-Night Diner"

Rat's Ass Review: "North Country Notes," "Wal-Mart Parking Lot, 2 a.m."

Red-Eft Review: "The Electric Bakery"

Right-Hand Pointing: "Helen," "The Sound of Spring"

The MacGuffin: "At the Odeon, 1969"

Third Wednesday: "Passing Through Nelma, WI"

Contents

Passing through Nelma, Wi.

Small towns pass into
the rearview mirror
from Anvil Lake to Iron River.

Shuttered hardware stores
and two-pump gas stations
recede into pine-thick forests.

Telephone poles come staggering
along the road, crossbars
broken, no pole straight.

At the last bend before
Michigan a weedy
field surrounds a silo,

sagging and roofless.
Suddenly an intersection
of gray abandonment:

shadows of buildings, rusted
pickups, a trailer home with broken
windows of somebody's life.

Solitary at the end of a vanishing
perspective, the failing neon
of the Triangle Tavern blinks

"open" in the old language.

Memorial Day Parade, Wisconsin, 1970

We started in the drizzle next to the old
train depot on Doty Island. In our full
khaki, badges, and sashes, Boy Scout
Troop 43 was set to march.

The Neenah High School Band went first,
strutting down Commercial Street in red
sweaters and berets, playing Sousa.

We fell in line behind the American Legion
and VFW. Terry, Mike, Greg; thirty of us
in formation, me out front with that heavy
flag in the leather harness, held forward
at the exact right angle. Mark carried
the state flag on my left.

The Horace Mann Middle School Band
struck up *America the Beautiful* behind us.
Then the Boy's Brigade, Rotarians, Elks,
and Knights of Columbus on their star-
spangled floats. Fire engines and pumper
trucks with lights on and horns blowing.

We passed Brazee's Hardware, the Ford
dealership, Sammy's Pizza, and over
the Fox River all the way into downtown.

Drumrolls, rim shots, trumpets blaring!
Bystanders clapping from both sides
of the rain-drenched street.

We could do anything after this. No gray
day could dampen the feeling. Such joy
seems unimaginable until I remember it.

On through the center of town and Main Street,
our heads and flags high, past waving, smiling, cheering.
Hamburgers and hot dogs in the church basement.

Walking home later filled with it still.

Cub Scout Pinewood Derby

Saturday morning boys
with miniature race cars
hope that gravity

will guide them to glory
on a downhill track.
Den mothers control

the chaos and the milk
and cookies. Fathers with
cups of coffee eye each

other's handiwork.
Russ shows off his orange
and black striped "Torpedo,"

Tim beams with his "Green
Hornet," Kevin is proud
of "Red Rocket." Wheels

tilted to decrease friction, axles
coated with graphite, weight
forward to give gravity a push.

Pray, then race.

Heats won, heats lost,
axles lock, wheels fall off,
cars spin out.

Driving Up North

Summer farms and fields
swept past my front seat world
in the Country Squire.

Mom and the rest dozed in the back.
Never in a hurry, Dad cruised
below the speed limit.

I twiddled with the AM radio to pull
in the Saturday game. The crackling signal
faded in and out.

Our winless team managed to score.
"College football's full of surprises!"
Dad slapped my shoulder.

We pulled over at the blinking neon
of Bob's Drive-In to "answer
the call of nature."

Drying my hands on my jeans,
the door to the grimy, soapless
bathroom scraped and closed.

Dad talked smart with the young waitress.
She filled his dented thermos with
a shy, nervous laugh.

Winking, his hand on my shoulder,
"Let's hit the road, kiddo."
Back on the highway,

everyone still asleep. I smelled the burned
black coffee in the cup I held for him.
It was heaven.

At the Odeon, 1969

Yellow neon lights, red velvet curtains,
cracked leather seats. Every Friday night
a new movie. Kids out from under their

parents for a summer evening and everyone
was there, friends, bullies throwing popcorn.
Flush with lawn mowing cash, joyously

splurging on Milky Ways, Necco wafers.
Chomping in the dark. First, a newsreel.
Watching, wide-eyed, we were the astronauts

on the moon, soldiers fighting in a jungle.
Later, we were John Wayne in *True Grit,*
and the girl who took the snake bite

like a trooper. Afterward, dazed in that
instant of transition, lost in the blackness,
the Odeon marquee shutting down behind us,

car lights sweeping away. We trudged home
quiet, thinking of toughness, good and evil,
persistence and loyalty. I wonder whatever

happened to those days, gone with the theater,
gone with the evenings when a ten-year-old
could go downtown and walk back in the dark.

Saturday Night Baseball

The crack of the bat holds
the strongest memory.
Under the lights the hometown
Zephyrs, no more athletic

than our recess bunch, last
in the league, but still
unmistakably baseball
and all that is summer.

If you were a kid this is where
you'd be, the air excitement,
possibility. Baseball was just
the sideshow. Fresca, hot dogs,

frozen Milky Ways. Hanging
out at the backstop. Your friends,
your new bike. The latest news:
Greg's dad home on leave,

Bruce's camping trip, then
unwanted details about your
delinquent brother. Now, the team
is losing again. The new girl

you've been dreaming about
is there somewhere but you can't
find her, and if you could she'd
probably be with some jerk

with muscles. Ice cream truck
arrives. Everyone runs to meet it,
but you don't even care,
your head's tired, a stone atop

a tendril, you just want to go
home. Then, sure enough, that
sound, fly ball over the fence,
the winning run for your home team.

Love in Hindsight

High school and,
finally talking to
the girl,
expecting electricity,
feeling none.

Another girl, who
years later is love,
a sweetheart for life,
at the same moment,
sits just behind you,
waiting.

Helen

"Don't you miss out on bein' alive,"
my southern grandmother said,

her gnarled fingers holding old moments:
the lost family farm, early widowhood,

dead children, and her one-room life
at a hundred years in her eyes like

the light of an uncertain candle.

At the Ojibwa All-Night Diner

Nothing else open this time of night
between Spooner and Woodruff. Old man
and woman shuffle to the first table. Worn
wood chairs scrape across the chipped

linoleum floor as they sit. Waitress
scribbles on her green pad, jet black eyes
and hair, and teenage resignation. Fry cook
father slumps in his chair and reads

a newspaper. Kitchen bell interrupts Hank
Williams belting *"I'm So Lonesome I
Could Cry"* on the chrome and neon Wurlitzer.
Old man steadies his sandwich, probably

a cold ham and cheese on whole wheat
with mustard and onion but no pickle,
carefully cuts it corner to corner, silently
slides one half onto his wife's plate as she

wearily adjusts her glasses and unrolls
a napkin. Hank's voice wails: *"Did you ever
see a night so slow as time goes draggin' by?
I'm so lonesome I could cry."*

North Country Notes

Eyeing the heavy clouds,
I said to the guide, I could
have picked a better day
to fish. He replied,
maybe so.

What's our weather look
like, I ask. It might rain,
he says, then again it
might not.

What about our luck today?
Could be good, he tells me,
could be bad.

I am home. Among my people,
What happens, happens.

At a Bend in the Road

At a bend in the road
a fallen fence, chained
gate, faded farmhouse.

Empty corncribs shudder
together before the north wind.

Near the once-red barn
and rusted pickup, no tracks.

An old farmer splits wood
on a battered stump, his

frayed flannel, blood
against the covering snow.

Maybe in spring there will be flowers.

The Electric Bakery, Park Falls, Wi.

Tonight I wonder about
the woman who used to visit

the bakery before the mill
closed, the bakery with it.

She picked her way down the cracked
sidewalk with her cane, same time

every morning. *Her husband
loved crullers,* the clerk said,

offering me a Bismarck instead.
We save the last one for her.

Wal-Mart Parking Lot, 2 A.M.

Decongestants, lozenges,
numbing spray. Street lights,
black pavement.

Three motorcycles, twenty-
something rider dudes.

A dented Honda Civic, door
open, dim yellow light.

Young mother faces defiant
young man. Baby in her arms,
no pajamas. She's pleading,
crying.

Cycles roar, tires squeal.
Car door slams.

My drive home, full moon
a white beacon on the water.
Two geese swimming side by side.

Early Sunday Morning

Across from the coffee shop a bus
stops, discharges a single passenger,
a man with a suitcase and cane. He looks
left, then right, slowly disappears around

the corner. My walk home, the two-block
downtown nearly empty. Fall wind off
the river gusting paper and leaves.
In front of the library, a woman

sitting on a bench, covered in her
belongings. One afternoon she
appeared at the bus stop, three suitcases,
two coats, no name. She dragged

her life and incoherent mutterings
from one end of town to the other,
back to the library bench each night.
Embraced by the town like a lost

relative, she accepted food, clothing,
money, but declined shelter, church
invitations, job offers. I hand
her my coffee. The hard creases

between her eyes almost vanish, now
like anybody's mother, soft-faced, silent,
gentle. She and her suitcases were last
seen at the bus stop a few days later.

At the Polling Place

In the early spring
wind the flag snaps
and tugs at the pole
beside the door

of the old boathouse,
repurposed for our
civic duty. Mid-day
voters form a line

to enter. Suits, uniforms,
walkers. Murmurs
of a late spring snow.
A dog sleeps inside

the door. Name and
address triple checked
at a table decorated
with red, white, and blue.

Gray-haired volunteers
remember my parents.
I darken the circles
for a slate of candidates

and approve the school
referendum. At the exit,
handshakes, a percolator
of coffee, a stack of cups,

a sign reading,
"Poll Workers Only."
Inducements for voters
are not permitted,

I am told. Outside
the flag pulley clinks
on the pole. Across
the river the red

brick faces of the
library and town hall.
Beyond stretches the
Republic I love.

The Corner Store

Clumps of peonies along the storefront,
deep heads heavy as fruit, drooping

in the summer sun. The front door
an immaculate white. A bell rings entrance.

An old freezer, full of ice cream sandwiches
and popsicles, mumbles along. Boxes

of fresh apples, oranges, bananas
on the floor, luminous and exotic.

Near the front window, bins of candy,
wondrously multicolored. A gum ball

machine at attention. Allowance
in my pocket begging to be spent.

The worn wooden floor creaks. I take
what I need from the narrow aisles.

Milk and eggs. Chops cut for tonight's
dinner, wrapped in brown butcher paper,

tied with string. The owner's wife smiles
a greeting. Through the back door, a living

room, the smell of coffee, a television
tuned to a game show. Years later,

no grocery sign, the white door entrance
now a picture window. A grandchild's swing

set and bicycle in the front yard.
Peonies still bright in the summer sun.

The Sound of Spring

I recall a blackbird
perched on our chimney,

and the melting snow,
and the ice gone overnight,
and the homecoming

of mallards, mergansers,
goldeneyes, and geese
to the open river,

and the end of the slowed
season with neighbors
now out of their houses,

this blackbird

warming herself and singing
to a mate in the treetops
and down the chimney to me,

not exactly the bird
but the cleansing
rains and green maple
days that followed her.

About the Author

Fredric Hildebrand lives in Neenah, WI, and began writing poetry after retiring from medical practice. His recent work has appeared in *Right-Hand Pointing* and *The Raven Review*. When not writing or reading he plays acoustic guitar and explores the Northwoods with his wife and two Labrador retrievers.

www.ingramcontent.com/pod-product-compliance
Lightning Source LLC
Chambersburg PA
CBHW031155090426
42738CB00008B/1352